Beautiful People
Beautiful Problems

Santosh Swaraj

BookLeaf Publishing

India | USA | UK

Made with ❤ on the BookLeaf Publishing Platform
www.bookleafpub.in
www.bookleafpub.com

Dedication

To those who are emotional and empathetic, who feel things deeply and differently.
To those who are mediocre, yet a rare gemstone, who carry the weight of world in their hearts and still find the strength to keep going!

Preface

" Beautiful people Beautiful problems" is born from life experiences, quiet struggles, silent storms and unspoken truths that so many carry within. Life is both beauty and burden, moments of highs and lows. These poems are reflection of inner battles and songs of hope. These verses are honest and right out of heart with first hand experiences.

Acknowledgements

This book came to the rescue when I was in a space of reluctance and reserved thoughts. It motivated me to brush off those fogs and helped me dived into creative world.

To my papa who has been my constant inspiration, his struggles never came in the way of love and protection he offered to the family. His genuine personality and kind heart encourages me to become a better person.

To the life itself, with all the beauty struggles and unpredictability!

1. Inconsequential

Choas follows enticing
While unadorned remains at peace
Amidst of a bustling city
When spotted a peacock
Fascinates bystander
Leading itself snatched
From the peace it had
While a pigeon
Common as muck
Dances free spirited
Makes whoope of life
Does that beguiling nature
Really easy to live with
Or its better
When you are left with no onlookers
Glum of being mediocre
Might convince you a cipher
Though it lets you enjoy
Your small wins and diminution

2. Little Things

Gush of air
That takes my worries away
Oh my sweats shines like a diamond !
Reflections of glazing sun.
Honks and maze of lanes
Struggling and crawling through
Each one of them
Found myself stranded
With red lights on each crossings
Little things a win.
Little things a pain.

Weird but sweet
After first rain
That nostalgic smell of soil
Brings back good ol memories
Oh that soothes !
Hot cup of tea biscuits aside
Would liked it dipped one at a time
Love so strong
That it chose to die
Oh that frustrates !
Little things a joy.
Little things a vain.

3. Truth of lies

Truth behind
The shadows of lies
Does it prevails?
Or does it dies?

Fake smiles and concerns
Makes you think little of yourself
Around struggle the one
Around success a bunch
Blaming you trying so hard
Humbles you with a victim card
How many cards yet to show?
Till I get the real you.
Conceited cocksure drunken ego
What is the truth?
What is a lie?

4. How hard it can be

Being grown up in a middle class setup
When toothpaste was just counting its last breath
How hard it can be?

Being exhausted by working
Seven hours a day
Coming back home with
A broad smile on face
How hard it can be?
For a man to put up with four children
That often gets on his nerve.

Being frustrated and angry
With problems at home, at school,
With friends or with study
How hard it can be?
To come in full force at your room
But closing door gently.

Being short of rations and supplies
Fighting every day
To keep a balance in life
How hard it can be?
For a mother to feed a family of six

With most of her strategic ability.

How hard it can be?

5. Wounds

Of all those touch
That was bound to her fate
Touch of lustful hands
No matter how much a man is aged

The impressions of groping scenes
Still engraved on skin.!
Experienced a galore episodes
Of all those touch
That was bound to her fate!

A part of that subconscious mind
Sussed a vague evocation
Of a toddler wearing snow white kind
Getting kissed by man of diabolical impression!
That's an onset of a downer tales
Of all those touch
That was bound to her fate!

6. Essence of life

The essence of life
Is felt by some
But meant by none
What one looks when looking
Into the mirror
Is that just skin and flesh
Or soul that craves
Things beyond !
When rain patters
Does it binds you with nature?
Or does it takes you to another dimension?
When you celebrate
Is it for the sake of culture?
Or does it gives you real elation?
When you love
Are you hoping to be loved back?
Or are you passionate selfless mad kind?
Fleeting moments or enduring ones
Packed with joy or pain
Leads you to treasure
The real essence of life !

7. Firefly

I was four
When mesmerized
By the spectacular sight
Of Firelies
Glowing in the dark
Like stars in the bush
But now I am blinded
By the beaming city lights
Why is it?
Does the firefly chose non-ecumene
Does it find solace there
And shine bright
Or are they needed there
Where there's no light
Overwhelmed by its very character
I wonder if I can be a firefly
To feel just once
How would it feel
To burn for someone
Till you die!

8. Mother

Standing at the door
When sky is all murked
Waiting for her child
Agony just vanishes away
When the child touched her wrinkled skin
Even if she is left abandoned
On dying hours
She is a mother
And love for her child never dies!

From crawl to run
Toddler to adult
Every stage lived
Every step taken
Is backed by a mother
A mother knows it all!

Hormones at highest peak
With that big bump the clothes doesn't fit
Mood swings every now and then
Cramps and pain
All the trimester
Universe bless the womb
For the mother who carries a life

She is a mother
A creator of life!

9. Half-pie

Little bit of this
Little bit of that
Good at some
Master of none
No matter how hard I try
I can never be the number one

Mediocrity established
Smothers my will
To commence on risky lane
Once I gather all utter courage
Found myself defeated
By condemnation and sham

Implications of others opinion
Veers my life decisions
It's unfair
For it's not their decision to make
They say I am adult
But took away autonomy
They say I am brave
But took away my bravery
They say I am creative
But took away my creativity

With constant grumble
And disappointed eyes
I hope to get back at them
It may take a while
For I am a mediocre
I will take my time!

10. Amour

Waking up in the night.
Starlight gazing through the window.
My wallet is a treasure.
Funny I lose it every time.
Waking up in the night.
Open up the wallet and saw your picture.
The treasure is all mine.
Dancing under the pillow.
Now sleeping like will never wake up.
Your picture is under my pillow.
Like sleeping on your lap.
Lost in the cotton candy.
Waking up every night.

11. Bumblebee

Chained with comfort
Fettered with cowardness
Break the chains
Let be free
You and your consciousness
If the water is still
It's funny and stinks
When it flows
It goes places and flourish
Sweet pain of struggles
Satiates your being
No other great triumph
No better jubilation
When you stumble and fall
And rise Victorious
Like a bumblebee

12. Godmother

While growing up
In a batch of siblings
Having a penchant for
The one
Just how moon chose Earth
Caress and brawl with
In amusement and in blah
Finding each other
Cheek by jowl
Untill it's time
When bird left it's flock
To go-to places
Now the left ones keep
All those sweet recollections
As souvenir in her heart
Heaven-sent that one
Who left but never left her
Braced her against all the odds
Blessed that little one
To have a fairy godmother alongside!

13. Go on

There were days
When you die a little
Hide your weep
Behind funny smile
Smelled weird
Yet none noticed
When You weren't You
Opened the pages
Of your heart
For people who can't read
Left alone to sink in
With mess of your own
Times you gather yourself
And kept in going
And now is not the time for
You to stop
You are the chariot of your life!

14. Human no kind

Creator must be lamenting
For it created Humankind
The perilous of all
Blessed it with brain
Hands and limbs
Pipe dream of them prospering
Making this world
A better place to live in
But here we are with
Cross swords
Over frivolous matters
Of caste creed race and religion
Shedding blood
Over a piece of land
The land that gave diamonds
This humankind requite with
Dumps of dumpyard
Creator must be repenting
Of its creation
For it created Human no kind
The fiendish of all!

15. Letter adrift

I am writing a letter
To the younger me
Hoping it somehow reach her
Time travelling
I will tell her to stop
And take a breath
To enjoy a little for time being
Allow her to make mistakes
And take steps
She hesitated
Make full of her knack
And savour the life
I will tell her
Not to carry the baggage
Of others expectations
Not to get carried away
With others petty judgement
I will tell her
That you are enough
Life will be hell of a rollercoaster
Will put you on trials
You will be fine!

16. Good ol' days

Where are those days
When life was simple
When festivals were not about
Attractions of instagram
But it was enjoyed
In its raw form
When powercuts made us happy
And gave us bonus playtime
When we were content
With stargazing on our
Father's lap
When even the lengthy stint
Of train journey was fun
With maa's meals on wheels
When we were young and stupid
Fooled around laughed and giggled
Without the worries
For ensuing days
Where are those days
When life was simple

17. Sweet blow

A sweet little blow
Erased my confusion
A universal colour
Strokes at each corner
Of my like you were there
You are here
Scent of your fingers
Took me to trans
Open the lid and hope there is a chance
Writting my own story
Ain't no ain't no
Ain't no sinking you're
Giving a meaning
Giving a purpose
 A liquid in a bottle
Have no clue
Why I was here
A navy blue
Leaking out write it down
Each curve has a sweet memory
Sinking thinking inking
Just a bottle of ink
Blow the paper before it spreads out and fades away
A sweet little blow...

18. Attache

Bitter must not be
The near better word
For people of this world
The sight of vicious
Insensitive and ungrateful
Gives me jitters up to toe
When ageing parents are
Abandoned
For whom they strived
Nearly all their life
That fallen attache now smothers soil
Had seen it all
Their life chapter of happy and toil
At times kept the lady's shawl
At times safeguarded man's record
Saw their child coming of age
Lying at the dusty edge
That lifeless attache
Had more loyalty
It chose to stay.

19. Will you?

Will you find me ?
If I get lost
Will you hold me ?
When I fall apart
Will you watch over me?
When I ll let my gaurds down
Will you calm me ?
When I am in anguish shape
Will you hold my hand ?
When I anxiously cross the streets
Will you still embrace me ?
Cause I have scars that's scary
Will you still love me ?
Cause I ain't no rose
But the wildflower no one needs.

20. The one

Standing still in storm
My hairs all wet
Splash of water
Sinking through the skin
Yet so proud
Of the comfort I find
In solitude and lone
Untill the moment
I saw the one
In the carpet of mist
I felt something strange
The one sailed his way
Took my roots from its core
And vanished on count of four
Universe laughed at me
As I chased him pronto
Landed on the heap of love
Care and tenderness
That smile transpose me
To a different world
The grays turns yellow
Now I crave his presence
Even if he is present!

21. Perfection Imperfection

Tides are high sometimes low
Moon is full and someday none
Some night sky full of stars
Others with a veil of clouds
Some days bright and sunny
Others when rain is funny
Today's loss tomorrow's win
Yin to the yang within
Perfection of Imperfections
Life is a rhythm
Sometimes fast and at times slow
Take a deep breath
Go with the flow!

www.ingramcontent.com/pod-product-compliance
Lightning Source LLC
Chambersburg PA
CBHW070725160726
48003CB00006BA/2389